I0521055

THE LEARNING CURVE

The Learning Curve

Gary Haywood

INTRODUCTION

THE OPERATING STACK

These books were not written to inspire confidence.
They were written to establish function.

Each volume addresses a different layer of operation, but none stand alone. Together, they form a complete system for living, deciding, and progressing under real-world constraints.

This is not motivational literature.
It is applied mechanics.

Self EMS establishes internal governance.
It answers the question most people avoid: *How do you operate when no one is watching?*
It introduces self-management as a system, monitoring inputs, correcting errors, and maintaining baseline function regardless of emotion.

Mastering the Basics builds execution discipline.
It removes complexity where none is required and demonstrates that most failure comes not from lack of intelligence, but from neglecting fundamentals. Stability precedes sophistication.

The Power of No Debt addresses structural leverage. It isolates financial dependency as a silent inhibitor of choice, time, and decision quality. Debt is framed not as morality, but as operational drag. Freedom is treated as a measurable condition.

The Learning Curve explains why none of the above appear to work at first.

This book exists to correct misinterpretation.

People abandon systems not because they are ineffective, but because they misunderstand feedback timing. They mistake delayed results for failure. They confuse discomfort with error. They expect linear progress in a nonlinear environment.

The Learning Curve is the glue. It explains how discipline compounds, why correction precedes recognition, and why correct behavior must be sustained long after reassurance disappears.

Together, these four books form an operating stack:

Self EMS governs behavior, Mastering the Basics stabilizes execution, The Power of No Debt removes structural friction, The Learning Curve calibrates expectation and endurance

Remove any one layer and the system degrades. This philosophy does not promise outcomes. It promises survivability under pressure. If you operate correctly long enough, results follow, not as rewards, but as consequences.

G rowth is not linear. Progress does not arrive on sched-
ule.

Most people abandon improvement because they misunderstand how learning behaves under pressure. They expect visible results early, reassurance often, and forward
momentum without friction.

Reality offers none of these.

You do not control outcomes. You control how quickly
and accurately you learn.

That control, how you respond to resistance, delay, and
error determines the shape of your trajectory. It determines whether your effort compounds or collapses. It determines whether time becomes an asset or a liability.

That is the curve.

PART I

UNDERSTANDING THE CURVE

L earning follows a curve, not a straight line.

Early effort produces minimal visible return. Later improvement appears sudden, but only because the groundwork was laid quietly and repeatedly.

This misleads observers and participants alike. Outsiders mistake late acceleration for talent. Participants mistake early stagnation for incompetence.

Neither is correct.

The curve rewards those who remain operational when feedback is weak. Skill, judgment, and efficiency accumulate long before results become obvious.

What looks like a breakthrough is usually delayed compensation. Impatience flattens the curve.

Consistency bends it.

Those who rush abandon the load too early. Those who stay under it allow adaptation to occur.

Why Early Progress Feels Slow

Early stages are filled with invisible work.
Neural pathways form. Habits stabilize. Errors decrease in frequency but not yet in consequence.

Nothing feels efficient because nothing is yet integrated. This phase is psychologically dangerous. It provides maximum effort with minimum validation.

Many mislabel this as failure and withdraw, restarting the curve elsewhere, relationships, careers, systems, or beliefs.

Slow progress is not failure. It is accumulation.

Those who quit early do not fail once. They fail repeatedly by never allowing learning to mature.

PART II

FAILURE AS A TOOL

Failure Compresses Learning.

Failure delivers immediate, high-density feedback. It exposes false assumptions faster than success ever could.

When examined correctly, failure shortens learning time. It removes guesswork and narrows viable options. It clarifies what does not work, which is more valuable than speculative optimism.

Avoided failure delays growth. Unexamined failure repeats.

The goal is not to fail less.

The goal is to fail **cleanly**, **deliberately**, and **informatively**.

Productive Failure vs. Chaos

Failure only teaches when contained. Chaos teaches nothing.

Unstructured failure overwhelms cognition. It produces emotion, not instruction. Lessons are lost because systems were absent.

Productive failure occurs inside boundaries. Risk is known. Variables are limited. Recovery paths exist.

Structure converts mistakes into curriculum. Without structure, failure becomes identity-forming instead of corrective.

With structure, it becomes procedural.

PART III

ADJUSTING YOUR CURVATURE

P atience is not waiting.

It is continuing correct behavior without reassurance.

The curve responds to time under load, not urgency.

Pressure applied briefly produces noise. Pressure sustained accurately produces adaptation.

Patience is active discipline. It is choosing repetition over novelty and restraint over reaction. Those who master the curve tolerate ambiguity longer than others.

Dedication Without Delusion

Dedication is accuracy, not intensity.
Effort that cannot be sustained is not commitment, it is volatility.

Emotional surges burn energy but distort judgment. They create short bursts followed by withdrawal. Delusion promises payoff without calibration.

Structure preserves energy by aligning effort with reality. Sustainable effort outperforms dramatic effort every time.

Systems Over Motivation

Motivation fades. Systems endure.

Motivation is a variable input. Systems are designed to function under low energy, low morale, and high friction.

Progress continues when behavior does not depend on mood.

The curve bends when actions are automatic, repeatable, and insulated from emotional swings.

Design beats desire.

PART IV

OPERATING UNDER PRESSURE

C onstraint accelerates learning by removing illusion.

Limited resources expose weak systems immediately. Pressure strips away preference and reveals function. What survives constraint is real. What collapses under it was decorative. Structure survives where emotion fails.

Those who learn to operate inside constraint gain leverage everywhere else.

Decision-Making When Behind

When behind, urgency lies. Speed without accuracy compounds loss.

The correct response is stabilization first, recovery second. Contain damage. Reduce variability. Restore baseline function.

Improvement does not begin with acceleration. It begins with control.

Those who understand the curve slow down strategically
to move forward sustainably.

PART V

LONG-TERM TRAJECTORY

Growth is sustained by limiting damage, not maximizing wins.

Buffers, boundaries, redundancy, and recovery paths preserve momentum. They prevent single errors from erasing accumulated progress.

Those who only chase upside, experience sharper collapses. Those who manage downside stay in the game long enough to compound.

Survival precedes optimization.

Compounding Small Corrections

Small adjustments applied consistently reshape trajectory. Correction does not need to be dramatic. It needs to be accurate and repeated.

Over time, marginal gains overtake sporadic breakthroughs. Compounding is quiet.

Its results are not.

R eading the Curve

The curve never disappears. Experience improves interpretation, not ease.

Mastery is not freedom from resistance, it is faster recognition of where you are on the curve and what response is required.

Experts are not exempt from the curve. They are simply calibrated to it.

You Control Curvature

Outcomes fluctuate. Learning compounds.
Respond correctly to resistance, failure, and pressure long enough, and the curve bends.

Not in your favor immediately. Not visibly at first. But decisively over time.

This is not optimism. It is mechanics.

EPILOGUE

OPERATING WITHOUT ILLUSION

There is no finish line. There is only calibration. Most people search for completion, a point where effort becomes optional and discipline relaxes. That point does not exist. Systems either operate, decay, or collapse.

Neutral is not an option.

The unified philosophy across these books is simple, but not easy:

You are responsible for your internal state (*Self EMS*)

You must execute fundamentals before optimizing (*Mastering the Basics*)

You cannot claim freedom while structurally constrained (*The Power of No Debt*)

And you must remain operational while progress remains invisible (*The Learning Curve*)

This is not self-help. It is self-command.

The learning curve never disappears. Debt can return. Basics erode. Self-governance weakens when neglected. None of this is failure, it is physics, God's Law.

The difference between those who stabilize and those who spiral is not intelligence, opportunity, or luck. It is interpretation.

Those who understand the curve do not panic when results lag.

Those who understand systems do not negotiate with fundamentals.

Those who understand leverage do not mortgage the future for comfort.

Those who understand themselves do not outsource discipline.

This philosophy does not promise ease. It offers alignment.

Operate long enough with accuracy, and the curve bends. Not toward comfort, but toward control.

That is the work. And it does not end.

www.ingramcontent.com/pod-product-compliance
Lightning Source LLC
Chambersburg PA
CBHW071232130626
46555CB00004B/1949